Contents

I0048411

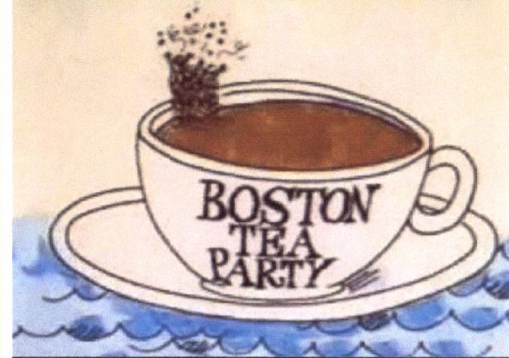

Contents

Women in RED

Life Worksh
& Tea
Ceremony

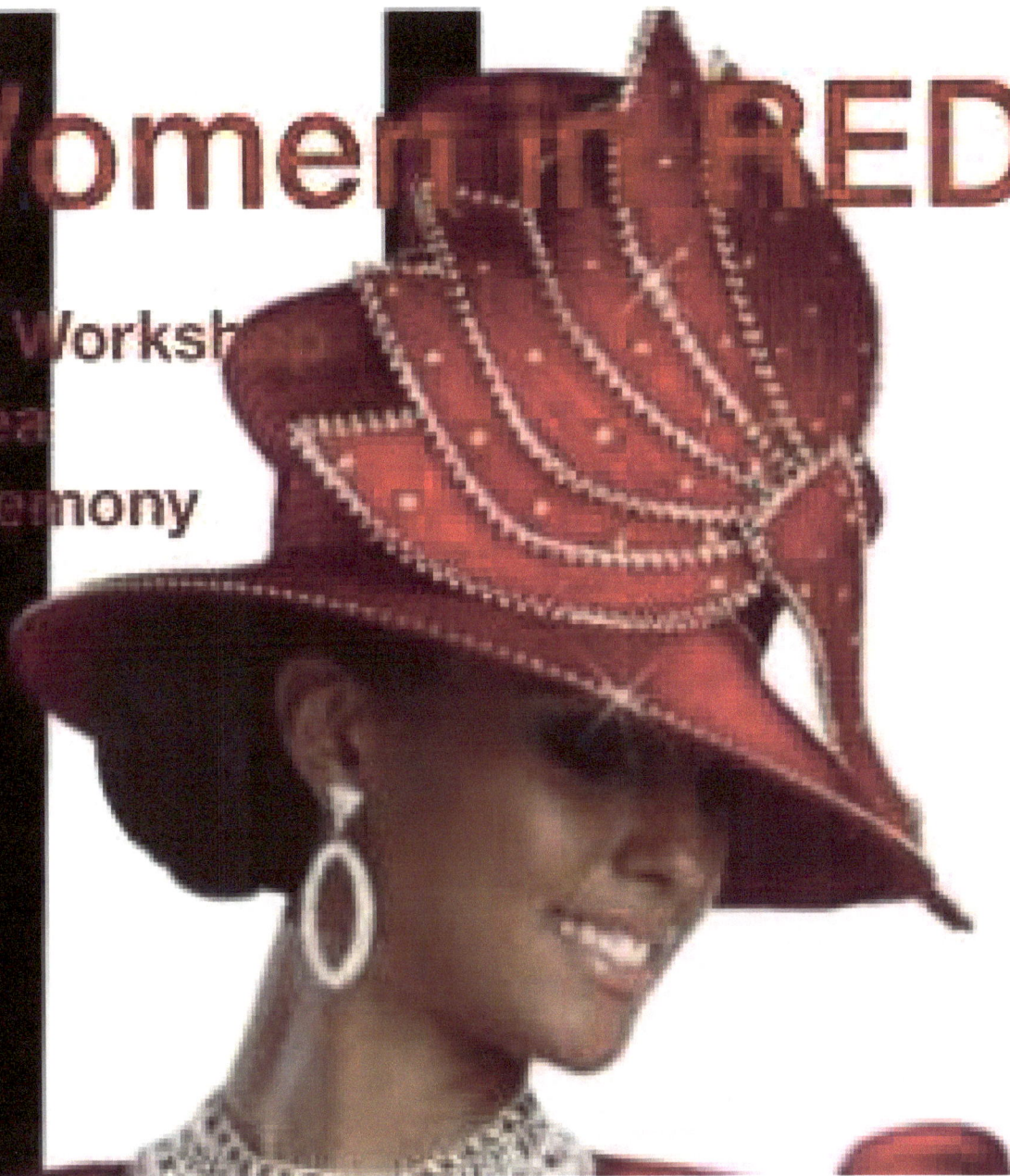

Women in Red

Hidden Gems & Jewels

Women in Red Tea Party

Hidden Gems & Jewels

Women in Red Tea

The Way of Tea

In a culture dominated by strong tastes, tea provides an opportunity to tune into more subtle flavors. Stress that a life of simplicity brings great peace. ... Tea not only serves as a symbol for a peaceful life but the act of drinking tea can provide the means to come in contact with it.

TEA SYMBOLISM

Tea represents harmony, peace, spiritual enlightenment, spiritual awakening, spiritual connection, rejuvenation, refreshment, change and contentment. The moment you sip hot tea, you feel satisfied and all of your stress is relieved. Dreaming of drinking hot ginger tea indicates happiness and good fortune.

Why do the English drink tea?

When people drank tea, they were expected to possess certain manners and behave in a particular way. ... Tea-drinking among these groups was also soon considered patriotic. Because the British East India Company had a monopoly over the tea industry in England, tea became more popular than coffee, chocolate, and alcohol.

Hidden Gems & Jewels

D BY FIRST LADY MYA S

First Lady Mya Stephenson

Hidden Gems & Jewels

Pastor Devin W. Stephenson

Hidden Gems & Jewels

Women in Red Tea
By 1st Lady Mya

Women in Red Tea was a ceremony about life. In particular, life as it pertains to us as women. The tea was a self-care and communal time to share with those who have made it to womanhood, are on their way to womanhood.

Women in Red Ceremonial Tea

It is also a way to remember and know thyself. The ceremony represents an ancient tea ceremony. 1st Lady Mya served three courses of tea, which represented the typical journey taken in the cycle of life. The ceremony represented the cycle of life and how God has helped us through it.

Our life's journey will be represented in three phases. The first course will represent love. This tea served by the first lady was frothy tea, which represented the good and the bad. Our second course was a sweet tea, representing the sweetness of life. The third course serving of the tea was bitter symbolizing the bittersweet times and sad times in life.

The women in red with through this ceremony together celebrating this journey that God has done through us allowing us to live the amazing gift that we call life. The tea was a symbol of friendship and goodwill. That 1st Lady Mya hoped that everyone enjoyed!

Elder
Stacey Bulluck

Hidden Gems and Jewels

What Does It Means To Be A Mother
Stacey Bulluck

Having the awesome opportunity to celebrate woman in a cultural ceremony is something that is rare and even more rare is to do it following the sacramental Attaya Tea. This tea is a critical part of building community relationships within certain cultures.

Mother's build communities

In this article I'm going to discuss a crucial component to building those who are in the community. Without the community there is no ceremony and a mother has a vital role to play in building and nurturing. This process of motherhood is like the process of the tea ceremony. Every African attaya ceremony consists of three rounds and as most of know there are three trimesters in pregnancy. All three rounds represent different stages.

The preparation of the tea, used in the attaya ritual, takes some time, just as it does to bring a child into the world. The amount of time needed in between rounds give everyone the time to commune with one another. Just as when a woman is pregnant it takes time for the child to come into the world, but when it does it is very familiar with one person that is the mother. Having these ceremonial gatherings gives those in the community an opportunity to become familiar with one another. There are many stories that speak of what each round means, but they all point to some version of "stages of life," and as we all know for the most part mothers play a critical role in all stages of life.

Mothers should take the responsibility seriously. Mothers have a unique and crucial role in the lives of their children. Motherhood is not a chore or unpleasant task. Just as a mother bears a child during pregnancy, and just as a mother feeds and cares for a child during infancy, so mothers also play an ongoing role in the lives of their children, whether they are adolescents, teenagers, young adults, or even adults with children of their own. While the role of motherhood must change and develop, the love, care, nurture, and encouragement a mother gives should never cease.

Duo Worship Leaders
Daughter and Mother

Worship Leadership
Prophetess Carolyn Ayers

Ministry leaders must be men or women of integrity, ethical and reliable giving the oration that is truth and directing their followers to a converted way of life that will enhance them and their family.

Spiritual leaders are not made by a formal group decision-making process or appointment. Simply holding a position does not make one a leader, nor do taking courses in leadership or resolving to become a leader. Spiritual leadership is a thing of the Spirit and is conferred by God alone. Spiritual leadership is a divine calling when a man or woman devotes their life to walking and living according to the well of God.

Skillful spiritual leaders will lead the followers. They will not be content for the people of God to remain as they are, nor even to manage them more efficiently. They will seek the growth of the people of God numerically. They will also seek their progress, individually and corporately, towards maturity. They will not be managers, for managers deal in seen realities, but leaders, for leaders deal in unseen potentials."

Leadership means to lead, leaders set direction and help themselves and others to do the right thing to move forward. To do this they create an inspiring vision, and then motivate and inspire others to reach that vision. Communication is one of the most important skills of a leader is the ability to communicate effectively. Awareness a strong leader should also have an eye on the business process to learn which ideas are effective and which are less effective.

Drinking tea has many natural ingredients there is green tea, black tea and white tea and they are infused with sweet and savory spices. Drinking teas contains antioxidants that comes from certain herbs that have healing properties that date back to African and Indian tribes. The English Tea party dates back to 1830's but there have been other tea parties, the Victorian tea party, Boston tea party, Garden tea party, Suffrage tea party, Political tea party as I researched each I find that they were talking about a small gathering of people mostly women.

These tea parties were about change, movement, making a difference for whatever their cause was to promote transformation, bring about new circumstances. Altering the present condition in their environment (atmosphere). I asked the Lord that our tea party on that night as we came on one accord bring a shift in the atmosphere in the body of Christ stirring our faith tearing down stronghold and bringing deliverance in the stratosphere.

Women in Red Tea Ceremony

As we come together as the Body of Christ in our Churches and keeping the Tea Party as a part of our tradition. Let us as the true believers of Jesus Christ continue to fellowship promoting change, movement, transformation and proper values in family, women, men and children.

Honoring the Word of God by teaching our young people to accept Jesus Christ as their Savior and enlighten them about their pass history and family values. Let the Red Woman Tea Party be an anointed movement of the Holy Ghost that will invoke deliverance, salvation and miracles that will change lives. I'm asking God to allow each time the Red Woman Tea party meet it is an Upper room experience.

By: Prophetess Carolyn Ayers

Hidden Gems & Jewels

WORSHIP LEADER OPPORTUNITY

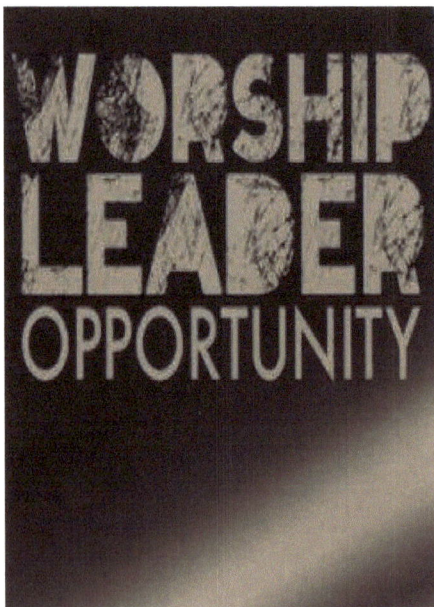

Prophetess Carolyn Ayers Bio

Affectionately known as Ms. C. by many of those who love and adore her, Prophetess Ayers is a mother and grandmother, a vibrant, energetic, woman of God admired for her humility, integrity, grace, and authenticity. With an undeniable passion for empowering women and young ladies, it is evident that God has called her to lead and be a "life changer" for today's generation. Prophetess is the founder of Women of Distinction Outreach Ministries and Reach the Press Publishing, an author and a preacher that comes with an in your face message about the love of Jesus Christ.

Hidden Gems & Jewels

Mrs. All About Me
Worship Leader

Hidden Gems & Jewels

The Queen and Princess
Mother and Daughter

Queen

A beautiful woman, who doesn't take disrespect from nobody! She's smart and does what she wants when she wants. She doesn't let nobody bully her and speaks her mind.

Princess

A girl who is sweet, kind, smart, goofy, intelligent, beautiful and an amazing friend to have. She will always be there for you and help you out with your problems and will never judge you. She can be a little spoiled at times but doesn't Bragg or even likes to bring it up at times. Overall princess is just an amazing person in general. She is also a bold and brave little girl.

Mrs. All About Me, L.A. Anderson, she believes in inspiring and changing the lives of others she is an Entrepreneur: launching Creation Essentials All Natural Body products.

Mrs. All About Me also sharing the stage with her sister by inspiring women through La'Shaes Events and Expos. She is a humanitarian creating Mission 200 Outreach feeding 200 families around the world. Mrs. All About Me is an author of a workbook and children books entitled A New Life Workbook on Amazon and Baby Girl children's books coming in 2019.
La'Shone
believe that change is at your door all you have to do is step out and your life will never be the same!

Tea is an aromatic beverage commonly prepared by pouring hot or boiling water over cured leaves of the Camellia plant species, an evergreen shrub native to East Asia. After water, it is the most widely consumed drink in the world.

Hidden Gems & Jewels

Trina
Cook Garrett

Hidden Gems and Jewels

LaTrina Cook Garrett
Gospel Artist

LaTrina Cook Garrett-Gospel Artist , Trina Cook Garrett's singing is exciting and breathtaking. She is noted for her mesmerizing and captivating vocal lyrics in her gospel solos.

Trina is a musician who uses her voice as her instrument, displaying precision and agility, mixed with heartfelt emotion. Prophetess Carolyn A. Ayers praised her dynamic solo renditions at the Alabaster Box Fellowship Gospel Explosion in Houston, TX which was both beautiful and touching. Her honesty shines in her well-chosen collection of gospel songs. Prophetess Ayers proclaimed Trina, "a gift from Houston, TX" expressing that her gospel solos are very penetrating.

Mrs. Cook Garrett is married to her husband Ricky Garrett and she resides in Houston, Texas area. She was the Praise and Worship leader at her mother's church, Fire Walls Ministry, Pastored by Pastor Helen Cook

LaTrina Cook Garrett Gospel Artist

Trina had the opportunity to sing with Gospel Artist Kirk Franklin and God's Property, Prayze Nation, The Remnant, ZDL and Phaze and more. Mrs. Cook Garrett attends Greater New Hope Church, Pastor Robert Bailey Jr. is the Senior Pastor. Trina is a member of the Greater New Hope Church Choir and the Praise Team.

Mrs. Cook Garrett was ordained and she is a licensed Evangelist she is a woman of profound intercession coupled with a passion to minister healing to hurting people. Therefore, she is confident of her calling and the work that the Lord have for her to complete

Trina has a single CD entitled (Worship Him). For booking, you can contact this amazing woman of God at tcg.ministry@yahoo.com

Hidden Gems and Jewels

Women in Red
Tea Time

Hidden Gems & Jewels

Green tea is the healthiest beverage on the planet. It is loaded with antioxidants and nutrients that have powerful effects on the body. These include improved brain function, fat loss, a lower risk of cancer and many other impressive benefits.

Green tea contains less caffeine than coffee, but enough to produce an effect. It also contains the amino acid L-theanine, which can work synergistically with caffeine to improve rain function.

Green tea has been shown to boost the metabolic rate and increase fat burning in the short term, although not all studies agree.

Hidden Gems & Jewels

Home Sweet Home

Hidden Gems and Jewels

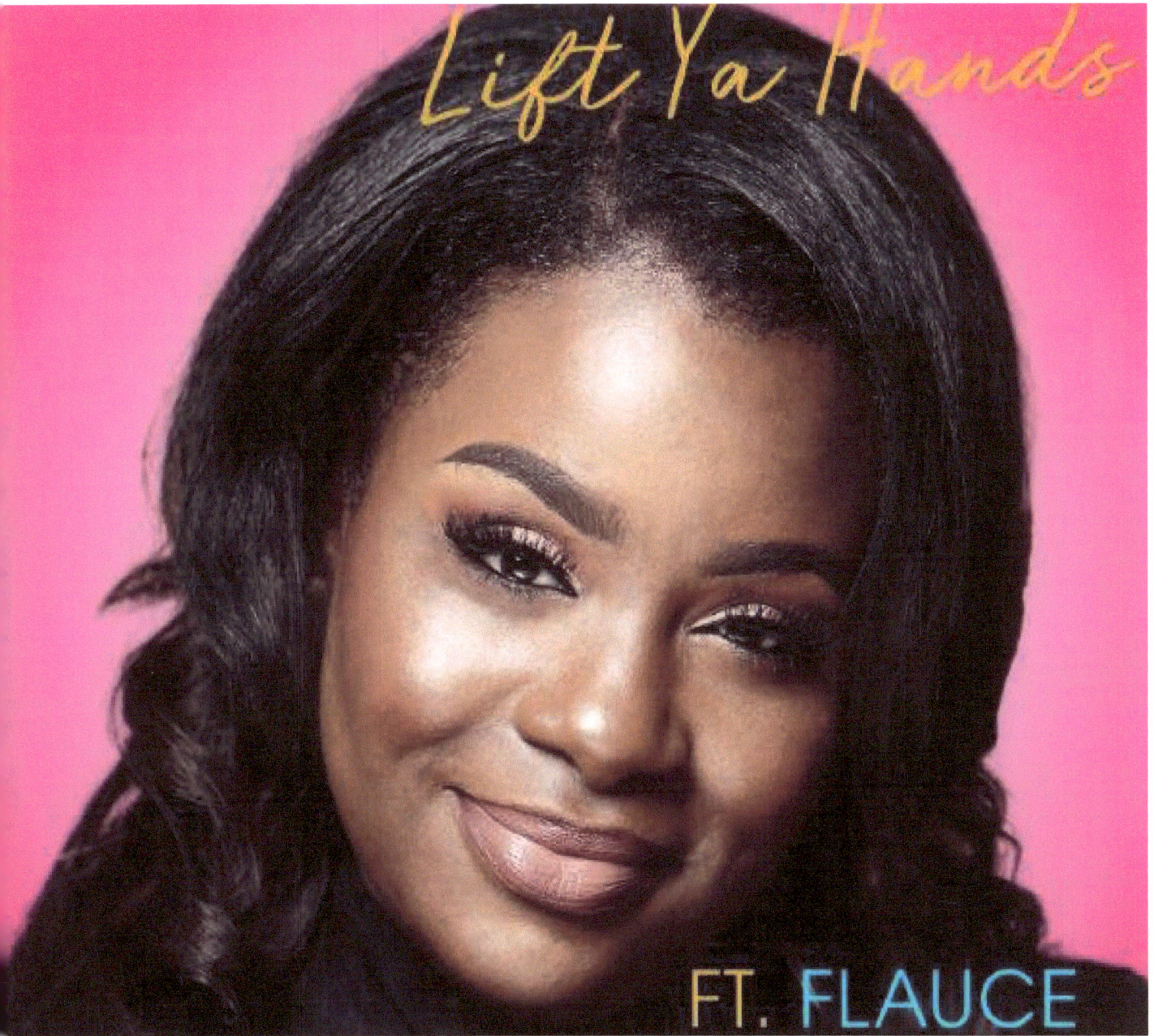

LaTonya Meori

Hidden Gems & Jewels

LaTonya Meori

L aTonya Meori is a dynamic Award Winning and National Recording Gospel Artist from the green pastures of Raleigh North Carolina.

She has had a passion for praise and worship since her early twenties, and continues to lead praise and worship throughout her region and nationally. She also exemplifies the heart of worship and strives to compel others to seek the PRESENCE of God.

In 2017 LaTonya released her first single Do The Impossible, which was birthed from God's unfailing power towards his children. In 2018, LaTonya was named ACHI Magazine's Songstress of the year for her region.

The Lord has also favored LaTonya to continue recording and releasing new music. She will be releasing her new single Lift Ya Hands, in the 1st quarter of 2019 on all digital outlets. LaTonya is quickly making a name for herself by seeking the wisdom of scripture and seeking the Lord's face. "There is nothing like the PRESENCE of God "! Please follow LaTonya Meori on all Social Media Platforms, she may be headed your way. God has abundantly blessed Mrs. Meori, as she is set to hit the road in 2019 for a praise and worship tour!

Ceremony
about Womanhood

Hidden Gems and Jewels

Elder Sheilah Olds is loving, loyal, giving, kindhearted and peaceable, and speaks the truth...in love. "A gracious woman retaineth honour..." — Proverbs 11:16

She loves Jesus Christ, his people and those in need of a Saviour. She is graciously anointed and was assigned by God in January 2007 to preach His liberating truths. She's received instruction from some of God's most greatly anointed Christian Education institutions such as the Perfecting Saints Leadership Institute at the Kingdom Worship Center, Towson, Maryland. At Dominion Church at Joy House Elder Sheilah is affectionately known as the Leading Lady. Her Spiritual Gifts are as follows: Voluntary Poverty, Helps, Discernment, Giving, Faith, Hospitality, Intercession, And, she selflessly and passionately leads other women and young women by example in being patient, prayerful and peaceful. Wow! What a gift and asset to the Body of Christ!

What Does It Mean to be a Wife?

"God wants us to be a helper. Help him to be what God has purposed him to become. Respect him, when you respect him, you are valuing his opinion and admiring his wisdom and character. Love, him and finally submit. Submit to his leadership as he follows after Christ. And most importantly, be his number one cheerleader."

By: 1st Lady Sheilah Olds

In marriage, there should be mutual submission.Man and woman being one in marriage there are no distinctive roles for men and women in marriage or in the church. There should be "mutual submission," with no one exercising final authority. The biblical commands for wives to be subject to their husbands as well as husband to be subject to their wives. Paul told wives to be subject to their husbands in that male-dominated culture so that the truth of the equality of the sexes would not interfere with the gospel. But to keep the home sanctified husband and wives should be subject to one another.

The headship of the husband is stated as a fact, but the commands to submit are always given to the wife. The husband is commanded to love his wife sacrificially.True submission is communicated both by attitudes and actions. A wife can be strong and even outspoken and yet be submissive in spirit if she respects her husband and backs his leadership even when she disagrees.

By: Prophetess Carolyn Ayers

Hidden Gems and Jewels

Worship at the Tea

Women in Red Tea Ceremony

These awesome Women of God came out to fellowship with
First Lady Mya Stephenson

Hidden Gems & Jewels

Michelle Boulden Hammond

Hidden Gems & Jewels

WHO IS TEAM M. A. B. B.?

Author/Coach, Motivational Speaker Michelle Boulden Hammond usually hosts women empowerment gathering quarterly throughout the year. M.A.B.B.

The word MABB stands for Mind, Affirmations, and Beauty & Boldness. This awesome team lead by Michelle Boulden Hammond was designed for the ladies to focus on their Minds and Affirm there creativeness and Beauty and be Bold to access the adventures in their journey to success.

The team consisted of mental health therapist Author/ Dr. Valeka Moore of Empowerment Thru Expression, Transformation Strategist Amina Carter, Radio Show Host of Dd Talks / Ashley Stewarts 2018 Contestant 8th Winner Up Diane Daiga and MUA Linette Michelle Howard of Extreme Beauty Studios Makeovers. The phenomenal ladies each gave useful information to help the ladies with making their plans to move into their now.

The room was filled with expectation and excitement. The host provided entrée selections of Latin Food that was outstanding and each lady left with a gift bag filled with trinkets for the mind, body and soul. A room full of positivity and authentic sisterhood captivated the room.

#Team
MABB

Mind, Affirmations Beauty
Affirmations

More Info on events or booking

TEAM MABB contact Michelle
Boulden Hammond 410-253-6937
beinspired70@yahoo.com

Hidden Gems & Jewels

I AM Free

Darlene Watts Howard

Hidden Gems & Jewels

Darlene Watts Howard Recording Gospel Singer, Songwriter, Motivational Speaker Natural Praise Ministries.

New Independent Gospel Singer, songwriter, and Motivational Speaker Darlene Watts Howard are from Ninety Six SC live now in Columbia SC she has been singing for way over half her life.

At the age of 8 years old Darlene has graced many with her soulful voice and style of singing. She was inspired by some of Gospels greats. Aretha Franklin, Mavis Staples, Shirley Caesar, and Dottie Peoples. Her parents were the late Mr. and Mrs. William Chester Watts and they keep Darlene in music mainly in church, where she began to take music lessons with Barbara Maranie from greenwood SC. She also has opened up for numerous singer in her area.

Darlene has just recently been nominated in Memphis Tennessee at Showtime Entertainment Gospel Music Awards for New Artist of the year. She released her first single in September of 2017, titled I'm Free to follow by her full CD titled Thankful released March 2018. Darlene is a member of the Mt. Olive Baptist Church Saluda SC under the Doctor Adrian Wideman presides. She is a member and lead singer of the Praise and Worship Team, and Mass Choir. Darlene focuses to help the youth and our senior's community, and also we feed the homeless a few times a month and go into the neighborhoods nobody else wants to and minister to all people.

Darlene Watts Howard is an awesome Woman of God all about Kingdom Business and her awesome real true spirit of the Lord and her gift of song is breathtaking. You can see my work own face book Darlene Watts-Howard and you tube same name. Darlene is currently working own a few collaborations with international artists and working own here second album.

Thankful

DARLENE HOWARD

DARLENE WATTS HOWARD

104 Sonata Ct Columbia S.C. 29203

803-586-8035

pookiewatts74@gmail.com

www.naturalpraiseministries.com

DARLENE WATTS
HOWARD

Hidden Gems & Jewels

Matter of The Heart

Hidden Gems & Jewels

LADY BUTTERFLY

La'Shaes

2019

In 2019 join Lady Butterfly and La'Shaes.

The Matter of The Heart Event. That is focus on marriage, family, and relationship. This is going to be the 6th Annual Event.

These amazing women have been promoting entrepreneurs and small business owners giving them a platform to showcase their talent.

This organization is all about inspiration, sophistication and motivations.

Hidden Gems & Jewels

Motherhood

Is a blessing from God, to put someone else's happiness and well-being a head of your own. To teach the hard lessons, to do the right things even when you're not sure how to do the right things.....Forgiving yourself, over and over again, for doing everything wrong.

Prophetess
Carolyn A. Ayers

Motherhood

Motherhood is unselfishness. When you become a mother, you are no longer the center of your own universe. You relinquish that position to your children.

Being A Mother

Being A Mother

The only woman in the world who will still cradle you in her arms even if you've stabbed her loving heart each time you've hung up her calls, thrown away her delicious food just because your friends thought McDonald was cool; got a failing progress report; told her to go away in the presence of your apparently 'cool' friends, ignored her for telling you to do your school work before play; taking juvenile revenge on her for only protecting you from the seemingly harmless evils in the world around you. Supporting your dream even when she feels it may not be the best for you and praying that it works out.

And still say she loves you and you will always be her child, no matter what. It's not just the placenta that forms a bond between a mother and a child. It's the mother herself who loves her child unconditionally.

Motherhood is a great honor and privilege, yet it is also synonymous with servanthood. Every day women are called upon to selflessly meet the needs of their families. Whether they are awake at night nursing a baby, spending their time and money on less-than-grateful teenagers. Being the scooter mom dropping you off and picking you up even when she has ten other things on her to do list.

Support the outreach and spreading of amazing stories and advertisement by placing an Ad or article in Hidden Gems and Jewels

If you would like to place an article about your business or ministry contact: Hidden Gems & Jewels Magazine CEO Carolyn A. Ayers at carolynayers@comcast.net

Thank you to everyone who has supported my magazine by placing their amazing story or Ad.

Hidden Gems and Jewels

Chief Executive Officer
Carolyn A. Ayers

CEO

Own the Vision

Provide the Proper Resources

Build the Culture

Make Great Decisions

Oversee the company's Performance

WOMEN OF DISTINCTION

Women Making A Diffence

www.ingramcontent.com/pod-product-compliance
Lightning Source LLC
Chambersburg PA
CBHW041452210326
41599CB00004B/225